IMAGES OF ENGLAND

Winslow

Midgley's ironmongers shop, decorated for King George V's Jubilee, 1935.

IMAGES OF ENGLAND

Winslow

Terry Foley
and
Julian Hunt

NONSUCH

First published 1997
This new pocket edition 2006
Images unchanged from first edition

Nonsuch Publishing Limited
The Mill, Brimscombe Port,
Stroud, Gloucestershire, GL5 2QG
www.nonsuch-publishing.com

Nonsuch Publishing is an imprint of Tempus Publishing Group

British Library Cataloguing in Publication Data.
A catalogue record for this book is available from the British Library.

ISBN 1-84588-338-1

Typesetting and origination by Nonsuch Publishing Limited
Printed in Great Britain by Oaklands Book Services Limited

Contents

Acknowledgements

The authors wish to record their gratitude to the many Winslow people who have contributed their photographs to Terry's ever growing archive and allowed Julian access to the property deeds on which many of the captions depend. Particular thanks go to Alan Wigley, another Winslow historian, who provided some of the more unusual images, to Jonathan How and Angela Grainge for photographs of Redfield, to Ken Reading for photographs of the 1599 map of the Salden Estate, to Donald Walker who supplied the photographs of Rands Farm and to the Wolverton Archaeological Society for permission to reproduce the photograph of the Winslow Commercial School.

Julian would like to thank Norman Saving, the late Ted Bull, Tom Kemp and all the other members of the group who studied Winslow and the surrounding villages in a very enjoyable series of evening classes at the Winslow Centre from 1989/95. Thanks are also due to David Noy and Andrew Kemp for their work on the history of Winslow, to Jeff Cargill for copying several of the photographs and to the staff of the Buckinghamshire Record Office where the Winslow court rolls, the Lowndes Papers, Winslow deeds collected by the Buckinghamshire Archaeological Society and the records of George Wigley & Sons are preserved.

Introduction

Winslow is a small market town on the road from Aylesbury to Buckingham, too near to either to have become a commercial centre but large enough to attract the agricultural surplus of the neighbouring villages. It is noteworthy for having been given by King Offa as an endowment for St Albans Abbey and having a tenth-century perambulation of its boundary in Anglo-Saxon.

The principal road once ran east to west and the oldest houses are therefore found along Sheep Street and Horn Street, whose names evoke the smell of livestock sales. The Abbot of St Albans secured the market charter in 1235 and carved out a market place from Horn Street and the Churchyard. He even laid out a New Town, once called Cow Street and then, more politely, High Street. His tithe barn, where reluctant contributions to church funds were stored, survives in Horn Street, but little remains of his grange at Biggin, where the manor courts were held, except a dried-up moat.

The town is dwarfed by Winslow Hall, built in 1700 by William Lowndes, the local boy who made his fortune in London and rose to be Secretary of the Treasury. His grandfather had made ploughshares and kept the Angel Inn in Market Square. How he must have shocked his contemporaries as he bought the farms on Sheep Street only to demolish them to improve his view towards Granborough.

The Lowndes family not only changed the town but transformed the landscape. Their enclosure of the open fields of Shipton in 1745 and Winslow in 1767 meant that all the land which the farmers had cultivated in common was reallocated and quick-set hedges laid around the new allotments. Furze Lane was created to give access to several small allotments; Verney Road replaced the old route to Addington and the road from Swanbourne to Buckingham, which had bypassed the town, was blocked in order to divert traffic through Market Square.

The old coach road from Aylesbury, which followed a Roman road from Quarrendon to Granborough and then headed for Buckingham via East Claydon, was diverted through Whitchurch and Winslow in 1745. This gave a boost to trade in the town, where the Banbury coach stopped at the Bell Inn. Winslow may not have been a significant market, but it was certainly home to a large number of wealthy professional men serving the gentry of the surrounding villages. At any given time there would be two or three doctors, several attorneys and more than one surveyor, all of them occupying large houses near to Market Square.

Central Government was responsible for the next major change in Winslow. In 1834, the Poor Law Amendment Act brought about the sale of village poorhouses and their replacement by Union Workhouses in the larger towns. Winslow became the centre of a Union and a grim new Workhouse serving the town and neighbouring villages was built on Buckingham Road. A Board of Guardians was elected to run the Workhouse and the Rural Sanitary Authority was formed in 1872 as a sub-committee. The Sanitary Authority was replaced in 1894 by a Rural District Council whose main legacy was the building of solid new houses to rent at Western Lane, Tinkers End, Demoram Close, Burley's Road, Missenden Road and Verney Road. These houses date from the 1920s to the 1950s when successive governments gave subsidies to local authorities to provide for general housing needs and those displaced by slum clearance.

The northern part of the town developed in the Victorian period with the building of the Workhouse in 1837 and the laying out of a new road to the station in 1850. The railway brought no industry to the town, but it did provide a route to London for local dairy products. The railway also made Winslow accessible to the London sporting fraternity who kept hunting boxes in the town. Hunting boxes were country houses where the wealthy employed resident grooms to keep their horses in readiness for their owners to join the local hunts. Whenever a large house came on the market, the agents stressed its proximity to the station and the town's convenience for the meets of the Whaddon Chase, Bicester and Duke of Grafton's Foxhound. The town's population rose from 1,100 at the beginning of the nineteenth century to 1,890 in 1861, but then declined to 1,500 by the Second World War. The growth of road traffic had hardly begun in 1935 when the County Council proposed a bypass. It was car ownership which made it practicable for ordinary people to live in Winslow and work elsewhere. The Winslow Plan, agreed in 1967 by the County and the Rural District Councils, set a population target of 5,000 and led to the development of the Magpie Estate to the north-east of the town, beyond the line of the proposed bypass. Recent changes in transport policy have made the new road less likely but it would be a great irony if the Winslow landscape changed yet again with a bypass following the ancient route of the road from Swanbourne to Buckingham which was grassed over in 1767.

One

The Manor of Winslow

Offa, King of Mercia, by a charter of 792, gave Winslow, Granborough and Little Horwood to the newly founded Abbey of St Albans. Prayers for the eternal soul of the donor were said daily at St Albans until the Abbey was dissolved by Henry VIII over 700 years later. This illustration comes from the *St Albans Book of Donors* and purports to show Offa founding the Abbey.

The precise extent of the land given by Offa was not known until 1993 when a copy of the St Albans Cartulary, with Anglo-Saxon additions giving boundaries of several Abbey estates, was found in the National Library in Brussels. The Winslow text mentions forty landmarks which can still be traced and includes the 'Swanaburnan', the stream which forms the boundary between Winslow and Swanbourne here at Shipton Bridge.

The compilers of the Domesday Book found 18 ploughs on the Abbot's estate at Winslow, but the mention of woodland suggests that this included Little Horwood as well. They noted nine ploughs at Granborough. This drawing of five horses pulling a single blade plough through heavy clay at Winslow is from the diary of Reinhold Rutker Angerstein, a Swedish visitor to England in 1755.

The centre of the Abbot's estate was not in the town of Winslow but at Biggin, west of the bridge which carries the road to Granborough over Claydon Brook. There would have been a substantial house here where officials from St Albans could rest overnight and conduct the two manor courts held at Biggin each year. The moat which surrounded the house and these substantial banks (probably of a fish pond) can still be seen.

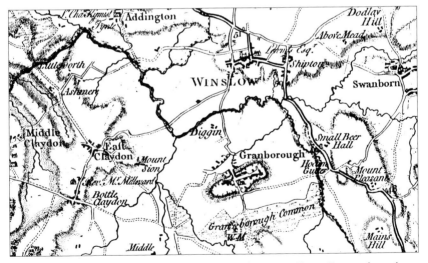

From a 1638 inventory of the goods of Stephen Janes, the tenant of Biggin Farm, we know that the house comprised a hall or living room, kitchen, buttery, best bedroom and bedroom over the kitchen. On the farm were 20 cattle, 19 sheep, 2 pigs, plus turkeys and poultry, and there was wheat, peas, beans and hay in the barn. Biggin ceased to be lived in during the eighteenth century, but the remaining farm buildings are shown on Jeffery's map of Buckinghamshire, published in 1770.

St Albans Abbey was dissolved in 1539 and Winslow, with the manor of Biggin, passed to the Crown. After leasing the estate to a succession of tenants, the Crown sold Winslow to Sir John Fortescue, Chancellor of the Duchy of Lancaster, who had a fine house at Salden, near Mursley. This map of Winslow comes from a survey of his Buckinghamshire estates made in 1599.

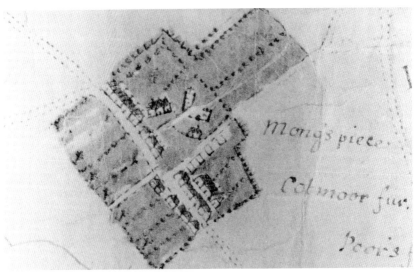

In 1697, the manor of Winslow was purchased by William Lowndes, Secretary to the Treasury, who was born in Winslow in 1652. He began to purchase property on Sheep Street in the 1690s, often at highly inflated prices, and in 1700 he demolished three farmhouses to build Winslow Hall. This detail from the 1599 map shows that there was already a large house or range of farm buildings behind the farmhouses on Sheep Street.

When William Lowndes' son Robert married in 1703, Winslow Hall was made over to him as part of the marriage settlement. As houses on the opposite side of Sheep Street became vacant, they were demolished to improve the view from the house towards Granborough.

Left: As Secretary to the Treasury, William Lowndes would have come into contact with Sir Christopher Wren, who won many contracts for public buildings at this time. It is not proven that Wren designed Winslow Hall but his signature is certainly on the surviving building accounts. This section of Winslow Hall shows its novel construction with its back-bone of chimneys giving excellent heat insulation.

Below: Winslow Hall remained the principal house of the Lowndes family until they moved to Whaddon Hall, which they inherited from the Selby family and rebuilt in about 1820. Winslow Hall was leased from 1841 to 1863 by Dr Lovell who ran a select boarding school there. In 1873 it was let to a London businessman called Henry Lambton who moved to Redfield in 1886.

B.H. LXXIX-A.

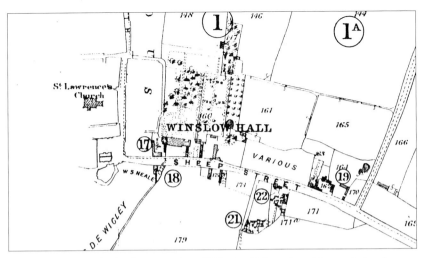

In 1897, the Lowndes family was forced to sell Winslow Hall together with an agricultural estate totalling nearly 1,400 acres. Winslow Hall was purchased by Norman McCorquodale who owned a large printing works in Wolverton. This map is from the 1897 sale catalogue.

The McCorquodales lived at Winslow Hall until the Second World War, when the house was requisitioned by the R.A.F. In 1947, Winslow Hall was bought by a demolition contractor, but, following a preservation order, it was purchased by an antique dealer named Geoffrey Houghton Brown. Since 1959, Winslow Hall has been the home of Sir Edward and Lady Tomkins.

The Abbot of St Albans had stored the tithes (a tenth of a farmer's crop paid to the church) in a large barn in Horn Street. The plot of land on which it stood was called Parson's Close. After the dissolution of the Monasteries, the Crown sold the tithes with the Manor of Winslow. By 1697, when William Lowndes bought the manor of Winslow, part of the tithe barn had already been converted into a house.

William Lowndes rebuilt the tithe barn about 1700, incorporating the tenant's house at the south end. When Winslow was enclosed in 1767, William Lowndes received a tenth of the land in lieu of his right to collect tithes. Enclosure made the tithe barn redundant and the living accommodation was gradually extended towards the central cart entrance.

Two

Enclosure of the Open Fields

Shipton was a hamlet of Winslow with its own set of three open fields called Licehill Field, Red Field or Varnham Field and Blackgrove Field. When one field grew wheat, another had a crop of peas or beans and the cattle and sheep were confined to the third fallow field. Every farmer, such as the occupants of these old houses on the Aylesbury Road, would have his land scattered in strips in each of these fields.

The Pyghtle at Shipton is a substantial farmhouse dating from the late sixteenth century. The brick infilling within the timber frame is in the then-fashionable herring-bone pattern.

Shipton was once a large and prosperous hamlet. The number of farms there was reduced after the enclosure of 1745, when houses like those on the right of this photograph became labourers' cottages. They were demolished in 1932 when a new bridge was built over Shipton Brook and Aylesbury Road was widened.

Another large farmhouse on the Swanbourne Road out of Shipton was occupied in the early part of the twentieth century by labourers working at nearby Rands Farm.

By the 1930s, the farmhouse had received so little maintenance that it was condemned and demolished.

Each farmer in Shipton ploughed his own strips of land in the open fields. The ploughshare turned the soil towards the centre of the strip, creating the landscape feature called ridge and furrow. These strips alongside Little Horwood Road were known as Peas Furlong, part of the Red Field of Shipton. Modern ploughing can soon obliterate ridge and furrow, but these ridges have survived because the land has remained pasture since 1745.

The enclosure of Shipton was brought about by Richard Lowndes who secured a private Act of Parliament in 1743, appointing commissioners with power to reallocate the strips in the open fields. His tenant here at Rands Farm was given almost the entire area of Blackgrove Field, immediately to the south-east of the farmhouse. Rands Farm is a sixteenth or seventeenth-century timber-framed house but the roofline was raised and the front rendered in cement in the early 1800s.

Rands Farm is named after Robert Rand who held the tenancy from 1859 until the 1880s. After the sale of the Winslow Estate in 1897, Rands farm was bought by the Fremantles of Swanbourne. These farm workers building a hay-rick behind the barns in the 1930s worked for Frederick Walker, whose father Alfred Walker leased the farm in 1907.

The most modern farm in Shipton is Red Hall Farm, a brick-built house with flanking chimneys, approached by a private driveway from the Swanbourne Road. It was built on 309 acres in the Red Field and Shipton Cowpasture, allotted to Richard Lowndes under the 1745 enclosure.

Richard Lowndes' son William had taken charge of the Winslow estate by 1765 when a further Act of Parliament enabled him to enclose the three open fields of Winslow township. The Old Mill Field was on the east side of the town, the West Field or New Mill Field on the north-west and Demoram Field on the south-west. This view, looking east from Furze Lane, shows ridge and furrow in the New Mill Field intersected by hedges marking the boundaries of allotments under the 1767 enclosure award.

At the time of enclosure, this fine farmhouse on Horn Street was owned by Thomas Blake whose family had run the nearby tannery. As a freeholder and occupier of more land than any other farmer, Blake's support for the enclosure would have been vital, so he was given 93 acres of land immediately to the south-west of the house.

The farmhouse was inherited in 1797 by the Jones family, who were farmers and lace dealers. They called the property Blake House. It is cement rendered, but the timber frame was revealed when, in an attempt to remove ivy, a recent owner pulled away the entire facade.

Because the land allotted at enclosure was so convenient to the house, Blake House remained a farm right up until modern times. It was renamed Tinker's Corner by the Countess of Lathom, who lived there in the 1930s. This photograph shows the rear of the house in 1968.

The 1767 enclosure award allocated 184 acres either side of the Claydon Road to William Lowndes in return for his giving up the right to collect tithes. In the centre of this block of land, William Lowndes built Tuckey Farm, which is approached by a private trackway from the Claydon Road.

Shipton Farm, a timber-framed building appearing to date from the sixteenth or seventeenth century, is not mentioned in the enclosure award, although it is in the middle of 162 acres in the Old Mill Field allotted to William Lowndes. It may well be that a complete house, or a set of used timbers, was re-erected here after the enclosure by a tenant whose old house in the town was not convenient to the new allotment of land.

The enclosure award gave William Lowndes a further allotment of 56 acres north of the Winslow to Buckingham Road. The farm he built here was called Dudslow, the ancient name of a group of strips or furlong in the New Mill Field. It was later called Mobbs Farm after a tenant named William Mobbs, but in about 1840 it was replaced by this country house called Selby Lodge, the home of Edward William Selby Lowndes, a younger son of the Winslow Hall family.

The Selby Lowndes family devoted a great deal of their time to fox hunting. The extensive stables they built to the rear of Selby Lodge are still standing.

The original drive to Selby Lodge ran directly from the south-east corner of the house to the Buckingham Road. Here was a lodge named Pettit's Lodge after one of the estate workers.

When Edward William Selby Lowndes died in 1885, Selby Lodge and over 160 acres of land was put up for auction. Newspaper advertisements stressed its proximity to the railway station and its convenience for the meets of the Whaddon Chase, Duke of Grafton's and the Bicester Foxhounds.

The Selby Lodge Estate was purchased in 1885 by Henry Lambton who completely rebuilt the front of the house and renamed it Redfield.

The Lambtons extended and developed the Redfield Estate, building distinctive estate-workers cottages on the Great Horwood Road. When the County Council bought Redfield for an old people's home in 1946, the land was divided into smallholdings. This estate cottage, which stands just to the north of the big house, became Redfield Farm.

Curtis's Farm, Sheep Street, with about 100 acres of land situated to the west of the Little Horwood Road, was one of the few old farmhouses in the main streets which survived the enclosure of 1767. It was occupied from about 1841 to 1858 by John Curtis and then by his widow Ann Curtis who died in 1901.

75 acres of Curtis's Farm was, however, split off for a new holding called Magpie Farm, built about 1840 and reached by an old track linking Buckingham Road to Little Horwood Road. It was demolished for the construction of the Magpie Estate in the 1970s and stood at the junction of the present Rudds Close and Magpie Way.

Three

Sheep Street

Sheep Street and Horn Street are lined with old farmsteads and form an east-west axis which is referred to as the 'Old Town' in early court rolls. Most of the tenant farmers were copyholders. Their farmhouses and strips in the open fields had no deeds other than a copy of the court rolls for the year they inherited or purchased their farms.

Sheep Street, Winslow.

Many farmsteads on Sheep Street became labourers' cottages after the 1767 enclosure. The large timber-framed house on the left became two cottages numbered 32-34 Sheep Street. One was occupied for many years by John Abbot and his son Edward who were parish clerks through most of the nineteenth century.

This rear view of 32-34 Sheep Street shows the results of multi-occupation, in that distinct parts of the old farmhouse were repaired by separate tenants using different materials.

These thatched cottages on Sheep Street were also farmhouses before enclosure. The little girl is walking past a cart entrance which gave access to the home close behind the farmhouse.

Several farmers supplemented their income by running beerhouses. These can hardly have been profitable except on market day. The Black Horse was run for many years by George Yeulet, the local carrier and coal merchant. It was later run by his widow and closed about 1926.

The timber frame of this former farmhouse in Sheep Street was covered over with cement rendering in the early nineteenth century. The opportunity was taken to replace tiles on the roof with slates, which can be laid at a more shallow angle, thus enabling the ceilings of the bedrooms to be raised.

The fine house next door is called Brook Hall, possibly after Benjamin Brooke, a currier (or leather worker), who lived here in the 1760s. It was purchased in 1786 by James Burnham, Solicitor and Clerk to the Buckingham to Wendover Turnpike Trust. Houses of this quality are usually associated with professional men whose businesses covered a wide area around a market town.

Four

Horn Street

Horn Street was formerly known as Great Horn Street and probably took its name from the cattle sales held there. This view was taken before the Congregational Church was built in 1884. The house on the extreme left was called The Limes and belonged, from the 1720s, to an apothecary called William Hobbs. It was bought in 1798, by Lancelot Wyatt, who took over from James Burnham as Clerk to the Buckingham to Wendover Turnpike Trust in 1803. The Limes was later occupied by Samuel Burnham Dudley, land agent and auctioneer. In 1906 it was purchased by Dr Kennish who renamed it The Cottage.

In this view of Horn Street in the early 1900s, the symmetry of The Cottage has been disturbed by the addition of a large bay window.

Houses like The Cottage must once have been farmhouses whose yards and home closes were turned into extensive gardens. Here The Cottage is viewed from The Walk. The house on the right is Sunny Lawn, an old house once occupied by John Clark, a carrier and maltster. It was probably rebuilt by John Tookey, a surgeon, who owned it from 1786 to 1827.

The Bull Inn was rebuilt in the eighteenth century, probably by Henry Burley, baker and publican, who had an extensive bakery behind the inn capable of baking 12 bushels of bread. His land on Western Lane was called Burley's Piece.

The cottage next to the Bull Inn was once occupied by an ostler and the outbuildings to the rear included stabling for 16 horses. The Bull Inn closed in 1993 and is now a private house.

Above: Next to the Bull is a timber-framed house which has been occupied by a succession of bakers at least from the mid-eighteenth century. Their names were Robert Blake, Thomas Bicknell, Robert Corbett, John Turnham, William Turnham, William Chowles and Cyril Beckett.

Left: William Turnham, aged 80, is shown standing outside the bakery in 1930.

A delivery of flour arrives at the bakery about 1910.

Cyril Beckett at work in the bakery about 1960. The Bakery became a private house in 1985.

Horn Street, Winslow.

The Crooked Billet, seen here on the left beyond the bay window of The Cottage, is an old timber-framed house with a late eighteenth-century brick facade. Successive publicans also farmed in Winslow; the large cart entry on the east side gave access to a home close behind. The Crooked Billet closed as a pub in February 1990 and became a private house in 1993.

Looking back up Horn Street, the fine red-brick house on the left had belonged to a butcher called Augustine Seaton, but the facade was probably put on by the solicitor Charles Willis, who lived there from 1810 until his death in 1845. The bay on the east end was added in 1829. The business was continued by his son, David Thomas Willis (1805-1884), one of whose daughters married Dr Newham of Western Lodge, whilst the other daughter married her cousin Thomas Price Willis of The Elms, High Street.

The Willis family purchased the tithe barn (to the right of the tree) in 1865 and let it as a hunting box. To the left of the tree is Western Lodge, occupied from 1835 by David Thomas Willis and then by his son-in-law, Dr Newham, who died in 1890. It was then let as a hunting box but was purchased by another doctor, Patrick Murphy, in 1949.

The large thatched house with a tiled gable on the corner of Horn Street was an old-established pub called the Plough Inn which closed in 1910. The cottage on the right was occupied by one of Winslow's last lacemakers. In 1851 there were 170 lacemakers in Winslow and a lace school was run in a cottage on the south of the churchyard, near to Yeates' Infant School.

Whenever Horn Street is dug up for laying pipes or cables, cattle horns are invariably discovered, suggesting another origin for the street name. This house on Horn Street, now known as Sunnyside, was once called the Old Tan Yard. Throughout the eighteenth century it belonged to the Blake family and was last run as a tannery by a relative named George Carpenter.

George Carpenter lived across the road from the tannery at the house with dormer windows, once called Emanuels Home and now known as 30 Horn Street. He died in 1798.

Horn Street passes between Blake House on the left and the stables to Western House on the right. Western House was a typical hunting box where the stabling was grander than the house.

Blake Cottage preserves the name of the family who owned the tannery. It was once separate from Blake House but was joined on to it, probably by the Countess of Lathom, in the 1930s.

Western House was built in 1859 by David Thomas Willis for his daughter Maria Louisa, who had recently married Dr Thomas Newham. It had 13 bedrooms and stabling for 20 horses. The Newhams moved to Western Lodge in 1869 and Western House was let to a Yorkshireman called Henry Greaves. Greaves' son, George Richard, married the Newham's daughter, Ellen Mary. Ellen Mary Greaves was widowed in 1895 and lived on at Western House until 1937. The house was then purchased by the Countess of Lathom, who demolished it in 1939 to build the present garages with groom's flat above.

Western House took its name from Western Lane, the continuation of Horn Street which was once the main road to Addington. At enclosure, Western Lane was stopped up and Verney Road laid out as a more convenient access to the enclosures on the Addington boundary.

The first council houses in Winslow were built on the north side of Western Lane after the First World War, as part of a national programme to build 'homes fit for heroes'. These houses in Demoram Close were part of an estate of 36 houses at Tinkers End and Western Lane planned by Winslow Rural District Council in 1946 and finished in 1948.

During the nineteenth century the road from Horn Street south towards Granborough became known as Tinkers End. Here were a few old labourers' cottages and a Victorian terrace known as Albert Place.

Claydon Road, Winslow.

Tinkers End is similar in appearance to the outskirts of several local villages where cottages have been built on the waste beside the road.

The Devil in the Boot beerhouse was also sited at Tinkers End. It is seen in course of repair about 1900. It had long been a cheap lodging house for labourers and those travelling in search of work, who may have given their name to this area.

Five

The Market Square

The Market Square appears to have been carved out of Horn Street and the churchyard about 1235 when the Abbot secured a market charter from the king. The fourteenth-century records of the Abbot's court mention houses, shops and a forge in the market place and even give the dimensions of some of the stalls, typically 12ft by 8ft.

Market Square, Winslow

Few of the stallholders mentioned in the earliest court rolls had surnames, so their Christian names are often coupled with their occupations, such as John the chapman, or chandler, smith, ironmonger, cooper, draper, tailor and shoemaker.

The Market Square would once have appeared much larger. The block including the George Inn is an early encroachment on the Square, where stallholders must have been given permission to build permanent structures.

The George Inn occupies the full depth of this encroachment on Market Square, but at the turn of the twentieth century there were three shops on the north side of the inn, those of William Turnham, confectioner, Richard Saunders, saddler, and William Jennings, signwriter. Jennings' shop was purchased in 1917 by the estate agents George Wigley & Sons, who put in a large bay window.

The part of the Market Square including Midgley's hardware shop is another encroachment on the Square. All the houses here are described in their deeds as built on the Butter Market. The early court rolls also mention separate cheese and meat markets.

The jettied building and the shops leading towards the Market Square are all of one build and date from the late sixteenth century. This house was also part of the Butter Market. From about 1815 it was occupied by a smith called Joseph King, whose business was continued from about 1830 by the Grace family.

The site occupied by the Winslow Fire Station was originally called the Pillory Ditch. The name occurs repeatedly in the medieval court rolls and refers to a pond in the vicinity which drained away towards Claydon Brook.

Right: An ancient road coming from the direction of Granborough and the Claydons entered the Market Square at Pillory Ditch. It was called The Walk, or Cowley's Walk, after the doctor who lived at Sunny Lawn. The photograph shows 3, The Walk, in poor repair in the 1930s. To the right is an old barn, formerly belonging to an inn called the Cross Keys, which stood here until the late eighteenth century.

Below: Number 9, The Walk, is an old farmhouse which may have been reduced to the status of a cottage when Sunny Lawn was built. The photograph dates from the 1930s.

In the centre of the Market Square was a market house constructed of timber, with stalls underneath and a room above for the Lord of the Manor's steward to hold the manor court. It remained in the Market Square until the beginning of the nineteenth century. Either side of the front door of 4, Market Square, formerly part of the Rose and Crown Inn, are two oak pillars which may have come from the old market hall. The Rose and Crown is the building with seven upper windows, three of them blank, standing in the side road to the right of George Wigley & Sons' offices.

All market towns have an abundance of public houses having the capacity to cater for all the visitors on market day. To the right of Wigley's office is the gabled front of the Crown Inn, an ancient hostelry which closed in 1896. To its right, the building painted white was the Punch Bowl which closed as a pub about 1850.

On the opposite side of the Square is another inn sign, that of the Royal Oak. This ceased to be a pub about 1910 when it was incorporated into Fulks' furniture, cycle and men's outfitters shop.

The sign of the Royal Oak is still in place in this later view of the Market Square. The building to the right with the new shop front was also purchased by Matthew Fulks. It was another ancient inn called the Angel, kept until 1654 by William Lowndes, grandfather of the builder of Winslow Hall.

The Bell Inn is best known for its association with the Neal family, licensees from 1810 until 1975. The building to the rear and to the right of the Bell was another old inn called the George. In 1821, the George was purchased by the Overseers of the Poor, for use as a workhouse, where the poor milled corn by hand. When the new Union Workhouse was built in 1837, the former George Inn was incorporated into the Bell.

The Bell narrowly escaped demolition in 1836 when the proprietor, Joseph Neal, fought the proposal to divert the turnpike road along a new line from the Market Square to Shipton Bridge.

The George Inn was originally known as the George and Horseshoe to distinguish it from the older inn behind the Bell. It is shown here in 1885 with the proprietor, Alfred Barton, outside the front door.

Cattle have been sold in Market Square from at least medieval times. The names Sheep Street, Horn Street and Cow Street (later High Street), suggest that livestock sales spilled over into the neighbouring streets. Early court rolls even mention a separate Hog Market.

From about 1820, cattle sales in the Square were conducted by Samuel Greaves Dudley who lived at 17 Market Square. He was the son of John Dudley, who had run the large drapery store (now numbered 15 Market Square) since the 1770s and also acted as a lace buyer.

The auctioneer Samuel Greaves Dudley married Sarah, daughter of the solicitor, James Burnham. On his death in 1856, the business was taken over by his son Samuel Burnham Dudley who lived at The Limes, Horn Street. Regular cattle sales were last held in the Market Square in 1898.

In 1875, one of Dudley's former employees, George Wigley, opened this cattle market off Bell Walk. Here his son Sidney Prudden Wigley is auctioning sheep, while William Monk of Tuckey Farm (on his left) looks on.

Left: The estate agent's business was continued by S.P. Wigley's son Alan Wigley, shown here on the right, auctioning cattle in the Winslow Sale Room in 1977.

Below: Wigley's sale yard, still owned by Alan Wigley, is now the only cattle market remaining in Buckinghamshire.

SUNNY LAWN
WINSLOW.

Above: In 1877, George Wigley was able to buy
Sunny Lawn, the fine house in The Walk which
had formerly belonged to the doctor, John Cowley.
George Wigley lived there until his death in 1906.

Right: George Wigley also built Prudden House in
The Walk, on the site of the old Cross Keys Inn. In
1891, it was occupied by a gardener and the market
porter, William French.

Some of the best houses in the Market Square were demolished about 1900. The three storey building with barred windows belonged to the solicitor, James Burnham jun. His family rented it to the Bucks and Oxon Union Bank from 1856 to 1891. The house to the left was one of a pair of houses belonging to the church. It was at one time leased to the lace buyer Thomas Yeates, whose daughter, Bridget Yeates, founded the Infants' School in the Churchyard. The bank and one of the church houses were demolished in 1891 to create a site for a new bank.

Whilst the new building was under construction, the Bucks and Oxon Union Bank moved to 4, High Street, later the premises of Thomas Saunders, hairdresser.

The Bucks and Oxon Union Bank was an amalgamation of private banks at Buckingham, Aylesbury and Banbury. The new bank at Winslow was built in 1891. The bank was taken over by Lloyds in 1903. The Post Office can still be seen on the left, dating this photograph to about 1895.

The ox-roasting to celebrate Queen Victoria's Diamond Jubilee was held outside the new bank. By 1897, the Post Office has closed but the building remains.

By 1911, the Post Office has been demolished ready for the building of a new hall called the St Lawrence Room. On the other side of the bank is a fine old house whose timber frame is hidden behind an eighteenth-century facade with Venetian windows. This was the home of solicitor Ferdinando Southam, Steward of the Manor of Winslow, who died in 1768. The house was subsequently purchased by John Cox. In the basement is a carved oak pillar, exactly similar to those used as door jambs at the Rose and Crown, which may have come from the old market house. Several more have been found at Buckslow Farm, Swanbourne, which was also owned by the Cox family.

On the corner of Market Square and High Street was an elegant shop called Market House. In the early nineteenth century this was a saddlery owned by William Mayne. After his death, his daughter Sarah ran a day school there, but from 1853 it was occupied by a succession of drapers, including Grant King, Thomas Sare, Charles Brown, Robert Cowper and Meanwell & Son.

Six

High Street

The entrance into High Street beside Market House was made even narrower by the extension of the shop front over the pavement. The new red-brick building opposite was the grocery store owned from 1794 by George Hawley and rebuilt by James G. Hawley about 1880.

The demolition of Market House in 1948 greatly improved access to High Street.

High Street appears to be the 'New Town' mentioned in early court rolls. The Hundred Rolls of 1279 give the names of 10 burgesses (inhabitants of a borough) whose houses would be built at the same time as Market Square was created. The shops on the right hand side of High Street are spaced at very regular intervals and each has a yard reached from an access road called Greyhound Lane.

High Street, Winslow.

Most of the houses on High Street are timber-framed, although several were cement-rendered in the early nineteenth century. The elegant five-bay house with railings was occupied from at least 1700 by a succession of doctors, including John Green, Joseph Turner, John Turner, John Sleath and John St Thomas Wynter. The building was refronted in the early nineteenth century when the bedrooms were raised and a shallow-angled slate roof replaced the steeper tiled roof at the front.

Parts of the High Street were rebuilt after the great fire of 1775. This started at the Three Pigeons, later occupied by French's stationary shop, and spread to Mrs Varney's, the house with the fine bay windows, at one time occupied by the Bucks and District Hand Laundry.

The fire of 1775 consumed the Sow and Pigs, later renamed the Kings Head, plus the next house belonging to Mrs Maiden, and also destroyed part of the Thomas Newman's Greyhound Inn at the end of High Street. This photograph also shows the Windmill Inn, named after the windmill which stood out in the open fields half a mile to the north-west.

The Elms, Winslow.

These offices were built in 1889 by the solicitor, Thomas Price Willis, on the site of a butcher's shop, formerly run by the Maiden family. The cement-rendered building with a small tower incorporates the Greyhound Inn, where the last publican was Fanny Newman who died in 1808. From 1828 to 1865 it was occupied by a tanner called George West. It was then rebuilt as a house for Thomas Price Willis who called it The Elms.

The former tannery buildings behind The Elms can be seen on this early view of Staniford House. A bricklayer named Richard Staniford bought the house in 1780 and his son, also named Richard, lived there until 1857.

The point at which the 'New Town' ceases was once clearly marked by the change in alignment of the road. On the left is Vicarage Road; on the right Greyhound Lane gives access to the rear of properties on the east of High Street, whilst straight ahead is Arundel House, once run as a commercial school by John Grace. The house belonged to the Matthews family, builders and plumbers, and the shop was let to the Northampton Electric Light and Power Company in 1830.

Vicarage Road was originally known as Back Lane, as it gave access to old enclosures or 'home closes' belonging to houses in Horn Street. It became Vicarage Lane or Road only after 1863, when the Revd Preston built his new house at the north end of the vicarage garden. On the right is Parson's Close.

Vicarage Road was not developed until after the Second World War. These new houses were built in 1951. St Lawrence and St Albans Roads were not built until the late 1950s.

High Street, Winslow.

That part of the High Street north of Greyhound Lane was originally known as Buckingham Road and was not built up until the nineteenth century. One of the few older buildings was the thatched house occupied by the confectioner, Frederick Benbow. This had been the parish workhouse until the new Union Workhouse was built further up the road in 1837. Almost opposite, behind the trees, was the National School, replaced by the new school in Sheep Street in 1901.

Frederick Benbow used to write rhyming advertisements for his goods and distribute them as handbills.

The Post Office moved from the Market Square to this shop in High Street in 1897. A small telephone exchange was installed in 1907. The photograph was taken in 1908 on the occasion of the presentation of long service awards. Retired postman George Wichello is in the centre wearing a straw hat.

The Post Office moved to new premises on the other side of High Street in 1911. This building remained in use until 1990 when the counter service moved to a sub-post office inside what had been Hawley's grocery shop in the Market Square. Letter sorting continues in the Post Office building.

The telephone exchange was also moved to the new post office in 1911. The telephone box outside the office was numbered 1, Winslow. The telephone exchange was replaced by a temporary automatic exchange next to Cantell's grocery shop just prior to the opening of the present exchange in 1969.

The population of Winslow rose from 1,100 in 1801, to nearly 1,900 in 1851. During this period, many old houses were taken down and new cottages like these on High Street were built. The Chandos Arms, shown here on the right, dates from 1839.

In the 1890s, these High Street premises belonged to Henry Ingram, plumber and china dealer, whilst next door was William Read's tailor's shop. They were demolished in 1973 to give access to Elmfields Estate.

This area of the High Street has seen most change, including a serious fire in 1933 and the 1943 crash of a Wellington bomber, which demolished the Chandos Arms and a row of cottages behind.

George Turner's drapery shop was destroyed by the 1933 fire, but Cantell's (originally the Oxon, Berks & Bucks Grocery Stores) survived. Beyond is the Golden Lion, first licensed in 1861, whilst the bay window opposite belonged to the Royal Engineer, first licensed in 1846 and demolished in 1959.

Avenue Road, Winslow.

Avenue Road was not developed until the 1890s. Norden House (on the right) was built for Dr Thomas Vaisey in 1891.

This terrace of houses on Avenue Road was built about 1895. The photograph shows the Rhodes family outside their house about 1906.

Park Road was laid out in the 1890s, when the terrace with bay windows extending to the first floor was built.

The large semi-detached houses at the top of Park Road were built in the early 1900s. A new Secondary School was built behind these houses in 1959.

This part of the High Street was for many years known as Union Street after the Union Workhouse, built in 1837. The large hip-roofed building with four chimney pots was the Railway Inn, owned by the Chesham and Brackley Brewery. It was renamed Chesham House when it became the home of the Midgley family.

Winslow's population declined after 1851, yet there was considerable house building in the Victorian period. The building plots on High Street were not developed in any particular order. These semi-detached houses were built in the late nineteenth century, long after the cottages on either side.

After the enclosure of most Midland parishes, farms became more efficient, less people were needed to work the land and greater numbers claimed poor relief or sought refuge in small parish workhouses. In an attempt to provide relief more effectively and to discourage all but the desperate, huge union workhouses like this one in Winslow were built in the 1830s to house all the poor of a district.

Winslow Union Workhouse took in the poor of Winslow and 16 neighbouring parishes. The building was erected in 1837 to the design of Gawcott-born George Gilbert Scott, later to become one of the most famous of English church architects. Only the master's house survives, the remainder of the workhouse having been demolished in 1983.

High Street increased in importance after the opening of the railway to Winslow in 1850. These houses overlooked the Union Workhouse. The Stag Inn was first licenced in 1852 by Charles Keys. He sold the premises to Phipps' Northampton and Towcester Breweries in 1895. The Stag closed in 1955.

The Swan Inn was built on the corner of Station Road, just as the railway was nearing completion in 1850. Three doors away, the house with the large bushes in the front garden is called Alwyn House. The Revd Preston lived there in 1863, whilst the new vicarage was being built.

New building continued along the Buckingham Road. On the right are Nevada Villas, built about 1875, whilst on the extreme left is the hunting box maintained by Sir Robert Abercromby.

Ribbon development along the road to Buckingham stopped at the railway bridge.

Station Road was laid out to link Buckingham Road to the railway station which opened in 1850. It soon became a fashionable address. The four houses in the terrace on the left had access through shared entries to coach houses at the rear. They were built in the 1850s.

The smaller terraced houses on the south side of Station Road are much smaller and have narrow entries to the rear gardens. Numbers 14 and 16, shown here, were built about 1905.

A new Police Station and Magistrates Court was built on Station Road following the establishment of the Buckinghamshire Constabulary in 1857. The buildings were demolished in 1984 and a housing development called Court House Close built on the site.

This large house next to the Police Station was originally called Claremont House, after the coal merchant Charles Clare, for whom the house was built about 1875. It was later renamed Northolme.

STATION ROAD, WINSLOW.

Most of the houses on the north side of Station Road were built before 1880. They enjoyed clear views over the fields to Shipton until the opposite side of the road was developed around the turn of the twentieth century.

Winslow streets were lit with gas from 1843 when a small gasworks was built on the High Street near the National School. A new gas company was formed in 1880 on a much larger scale. New gasworks were built at the bottom of Station Road, where the base of the gas holder can still be seen, next to the entrance to the station yard. On the left of this picture is Bellevue Terrace built in the 1870s.

Winslow was joined to the railway network in 1850 when the London & North Western Railway completed a line from Bletchley to Banbury, originally promoted by the Buckinghamshire Railway. A link to Oxford from Verney Junction was opened the following year. It is doubtful whether the railway led to greater prosperity, as no new industry came to Winslow and the market may even have decreased in importance when it became easier to reach Buckingham, Banbury and Oxford. The engine at Winslow station about 1915 is a L.& N.W.R. 0-8-0 heavy goods engine.

Here a Banbury train waits at Winslow in 1962. Winslow Station closed to passengers in 1968. Goods traffic continued, although the line was reduced to a single track in 1985. The line has not been used since a special train took a large contingent of local enthusiasts to Lincoln in 1993.

The railway station, being at the northern extremity of the town, was the obvious starting point for a carnival. Here the parade celebrating King George V's Jubilee assembles in 1935.

The Buckinghamshire Railway had intended to build a line to Aylesbury, but the L.& N.W.R. withdrew their support. The link was eventually provided in 1868 by a new company called the Aylesbury & Buckingham Railway, whose route from Claydon joined the Great Western Railway at Aylesbury. Winslow Road Station was provided where the railway crossed the road to East Claydon, offering an alternative route from Winslow to London.

Seven

Churches and Chapels

Church Street, Winslow.

Because the manor of Winslow belonged to St Albans Abbey, the Abbot appointed a vicar to officiate at Winslow. After the dissolution, the vicar was appointed by the Crown. The vicarage was approached from Horn Street via a narrow lane called Church Street.

This old farmhouse in Church Street was partially rebuilt in 1726 by a glover named George Barrett. The deeds to the house show that it was bounded on the west by the vicarage house and yard. In 1863 the old vicarage was demolished and part of the site was used for a girls' school, opened in 1865.

This view from the church tower shows a two-storey house on the left, with dormer windows and a porch, formerly known as Punn's Cottages. Some have suggested that this was an old vicarage, but there is no evidence for this.

The Revd Alfred Preston was appointed Vicar of Winslow in 1863 and obtained permission to take down his predecessor's house and to build a new vicarage on the home close behind. The tall Victorian building was approached from what was then called Back Lane but soon became known as Vicarage Road.

The Vicar of Winslow had always enjoyed the income from the glebe, strips of land he could cultivate himself or rent out to a local farmer. At enclosure, the Vicar was allocated a block of land at the end of Western Lane, where farm buildings were erected. The glebe was sold by the church in 1918 and bought in 1930 by Buckinghamshire County Council, as part of a national policy to provide smallholdings for those who couldn't afford to rent or buy existing farms. Glebe Farm was built to a standard design for houses on smallholdings adopted by the County Land Agent.

Like most parish churches, St Lawrence's, Winslow is a mixture of several styles of architecture, the earliest visible features dating from the early fourteenth century, and the latest being the vestry on the north side of the chancel, built in 1889.

The churchyard was hemmed in by Market Square and High Street so that the same ground must have been used for successive burials. Room for expansion was provided in the 1920s when Norman McCorquodale of Winslow Hall gave a piece of land between the Churchyard and Vicarage Road. This had been a bowling green belonging to the Willis family and was bought by McCorquodale at the sale of the Elms, High Street, in 1911.

Until 1884, St Lawrence's Church had a three-decker pulpit, box pews and galleries in the north and south aisles and in the west end of the nave. Above the plain communion table was a large board inscribed 'This do in remembrance of me'. All these features were the product of the English Reformation and had become unfashionable in the Victorian church.

The Revd Preston died in 1882 and was replaced by the Revd H.A. Douglas-Hamilton. In 1884 the new vicar pressed ahead with a series of alterations to the church which the architect, John Oldrid Scott, thought would restore its medieval appearance. The galleries were removed, neo-gothic benches replaced the box pews, the pulpit was made less obtrusive and the chancel was equipped with choir stalls and a more prominent altar.

Winslow has a strong nonconformist tradition. This Baptist meeting house was built in 1695 in the garden of a local draper named William Gyles. Non-conformist meeting houses of this period tend to be discreetly sited to avoid the sort of persecution which marked the career of Benjamin Keach, the popular seventeenth century local preacher, after whom the chapel is now named.

George Whichello, once Winslow's only postman, was also a deacon and trustee of the Baptist Chapel. He died in 1915, aged 94.

Inside the Baptist Chapel are eighteenth-century memorials to the Gyles and Norman families, as well as one celebrating the life of George Whichello.

A sudden influx of new members may account for the building of a small gallery on the south wall of the Baptist Chapel in 1827.

A small group of congregationalists shared the Baptist Chapel until 1816, when they purchased a barn on Horn Street. It was fitted out as a chapel, capable of seating 250 people. In 1830, the barn was demolished and this chapel, with seats for 300, a schoolroom and a vestry was built.

In 1884, a new Congregational Church was built at a cost of £2,400. The new church seated 240 people on the ground floor and 80 in the gallery. There was a Sunday School to the right of the entrance and a large classroom on the left. Prominent amongst the church's supporters were George Wigley, land agent, Edwin French, printer and Robert Williat Jones of Blake House, farmer.

The Congregational Church closed in 1989 and was converted into a private house.

An unusual feature of the Congregational Church was the large square tower. A spiral staircase on the south-west corner gave access to this small schoolroom at the top of the tower.

The Congregational Church had a strong amateur dramatic group. They are photographed outside Dr Kennish's house, The Cottage, in 1924.

Winslow has no old-established grammar school, although Joseph Rogers of Winslow, a currier, who died in 1722, left £600 in his will towards the education of poor people's children. This money was invested in land in Great Kimble and the rent payed to a succession of schoolmasters, who taught up to 20 boys on the upper floor of a barn situated behind these houses in Bell Alley. Thomas Rawbone, the master from 1775 to 1836, lived in the three-storey house on the corner of The Walk.

Yeates' Infants School was built on the south side of the Churchyard in 1841 on the site of an old cottage given by Bridget Yeates. She was the daughter of Thomas Yeates and sister of Samuel Yeates, both of whom were lace dealers in the town. She died in 1845 aged 67.

From 1841, the income from Joseph Rogers' charity was applied to a new school in High Street, supported by the National Society for the Education of the Poor in the Principles of the Established Church. Its first master was George Grace. It was replaced by this new National School in Sheep Street in 1901.

In 1903, Buckinghamshire County Council took over all elementary schools in the County, including Winslow Church of England School. Here members of the sports team assemble for a group photograph about 1910.

Winslow Church of England School closed in 1990 and has now been converted into two private houses. Three more houses have been built in a similar style on what was once the school garden. Headmaster George Pass and pupils are shown here in 1914 cultivating the garden.